The
WORST-CASE SCENARIO
POCKET GUIDE
MEETINGS

By David Borgenicht &
Ben H. Winters

Illustrations by Brenda Brown

CHRONICLE BOOKS
SAN FRANCISCO

Copyright © 2009 by Quirk Productions, Inc.

Worst-Case Scenario® and The Worst-Case Scenario Survival Handbook™ are trademarks of Quirk Productions, Inc.

Library of Congress Cataloging in Publication Data available.

ISBN: 978-0-8118-7048-1

Manufactured in China
Designed by Jenny Kraemer
Illustrations by Brenda Brown
Visit www.worstcasescenarios.com

10 9 8 7 6 5 4 3 2 1

Chronicle Books LLC
680 Second Street
San Francisco, CA 94107
www.chroniclebooks.com

WARNING: You really should have been more careful. Now you're facing one of the worst-case scenarios presented in this book—at least you have the book with you, to refer to. But you must use your good judgment and common sense and consult a professionally trained expert to deal with these dangerous situations. The authors, publisher, and experts disclaim any liability from any injury that may result from the use, proper or improper, from the information contained in this book. Nothing herein should be construed or interpreted to infringe on the rights of other persons or to violate criminal statutes. We urge you to be respectful and safe.

CONTENTS

INTRODUCTION

Is there any word in the workplace that inspires more dread than "meeting"? Artery-clogging pastries. Mind-numbing digital slide presentations. Lose–Lose jargon.

And don't fool yourself that those mid-day conference room confabs are only *time*killers—they can be shockingly dangerous. You'll learn in these pages how swiftly a discussion of best practices can turn into a minefield of worst-case scenarios, from trust-fall injuries to airways fatally obstructed by jelly doughnuts to a sudden need to pass gas.

Not to mention those sticky interpersonal emergencies that always seem to crop up. Your human resources department can't tell you how to expertly flatter your needy boss, or effectively stop a fistfight between a couple of coworkers. Luckily, we can.

Whether you're the one running the meeting or the one suffering through it, the *Worst-Case Scenario Pocket Guide: Meetings* just became your most valuable "team member." In it you'll find step-by-step instructions for how to video-conference from the beach, an instant solution for how to create office atmosphere, and charts on everything from characters to watch out for to a useful list of noncommittal affirmations. And when you've had just about enough, we'll show you how to discreetly duck out on the catering cart.

So the next time you're headed to the conference room, make sure to slip this little volume into your pocket. The one thing you don't want to meet is your doom.

—The Authors

The least productive people
are usually the ones who are most
in favor of holding meetings.
—Thomas Sowell

CHAPTER 1
INTERPERSONAL SKILLS

PLAYS WELL
WITH OTHERS

HOW TO BREAK UP A FISTFIGHT

1 Evacuate the room.
Open the door of the conference room and instruct everyone to leave. Tell everyone to stay in the immediate vicinity and be ready to resume the meeting shortly. Ask your largest and/or strongest colleague to remain behind.

2 Tell combatants to stop.
In a firm, authoritative voice, say, "Stop that!" and "That's enough!" Stand up on the conference table and repeat the order. Raise your voice, but do not scream.

3 Pour water on the combatants.
Pick up the water pitcher or flower vase from the conference table. Still standing atop the table, pour the water on the combatants while commanding them to

Chapter 1: Plays Well with Others

Pour water on the combatants.

stop fighting. Lukewarm coffee or cans of
soda will also work, but may leave stains.
Do not use hot coffee.

4 Disengage the fighters.
Approach one of the combatants from
behind. Grasp each of his arms at the
elbow and pull him away from his
adversary, while the large and/or strong
colleague performs the same maneuver
on the second combatant.

5 Stand between the two combatants.
Fully extend your arms to create a barrier
between them.

6 Brandish an office supply.
Wave a metal or hard plastic object such
as a stapler, ruler, or a laptop computer.
Again, tell them to stop. Do not assault
the combatants.

7 | Instruct the combatants to sit down.
Seat the fighters at opposite ends of the conference table. Give each of them napkins or paper towels to dry off.

8 | Take a "calming down" period.
Walk one of the combatants to the elevator and instruct him to take a ten-minute walk around the block. On the way back, inform the other meeting participants that the meeting will take a brief pause. Stay with the other combatant in the meeting room during the calming period, making small talk about nonwork-related matters.

9 | Usher other meeting participants back into the room.
After ten minutes, bring everyone back into the room.

10 | Resume meeting.
Skip over whatever agenda item sparked the fistfight.

Be Aware

- Warning signs of violence include surliness towards superiors, coworkers, and customers; frequent expressions of a sense of victimization; sleep troubles that affect job performance; and frequent use of inappropriate language. Avoid antagonizing people displaying these characteristics. If you display these behaviors, seek help from the human resources department.

- Before acting to break up any fight, remove your necktie or jewelry.

INSTANT SOLUTION

CREATE SPACE BETWEEN YOU AND A CLOSE TALKER

Turn away from the close talker and fake a sneeze.

HOW TO TREAT A TRUST-FALL INJURY

1 Deny responsibility.
Make it clear that it was not your fault that your coworker fell. Appear surprised and dismayed.

2 Form a circle around the injured person.
Kneel down and join hands with the other participants. Surround the person, murmuring affirmations. Exchange expressions of concern with your other coworkers.

3 Agree on who will perform various tasks.
Select one person to remain with the faller and provide verbal comfort, another person to check for physical injuries, and other individuals to seek blankets, water, health-care professionals, or legal counsel as the situation dictates.

Deny responsibility.

4 Ask simple questions.
Hold up your fingers in front of the victim's eyes and ask how many fingers she sees. Ask her name, the date, and her place of employment. If she appears disoriented or keeps falling asleep, call for an ambulance.

5 Sit victim comfortably.
Help the victim into a rolling chair with her head between her legs. Roll her into a corner of the room.

6 Check victim for abrasions and swelling.
Locate the area of the victim's head or other body part that made contact with the floor. Control swelling by wrapping five ice cubes in a necktie or scarf and pressing firmly against the injured area for twenty to thirty minutes. Stop bleeding by pressing firmly against the wound with folded-up napkins.

7 | Blame the consultants.

With silent, critical stares, convey to the trainers or consultants that the fault is theirs.

Be Aware

- Anyone who has sustained an injury to the head should not drink alcohol for 24 hours after the accident.
- If a coworker participating in a trust-fall exercise purposefully lets someone fall, do not trust that person in other work situations.

MOST COMMON WORKPLACE INJURIES

- Sprains and strains 38%

- Cuts, lacerations, and punctures 9%

- Bruises and contusions 9%

- Fractures 8%

- Soreness and pain (except back pain) 7%

- Multiple traumas 4%

- Back pain 3%

- Heat burns 2%

- Carpal tunnel 1%

- Amputations 1%

- Chemical burns 1%

- Other 17%

HOW TO REVIVE SOMEONE WHO HAS FAINTED

1   Lay the fainter on his back.
Do not place any cushioning under the fainter's head.

2   Make room around the fainter.
Ask everyone else to leave the room.

3   Open the door and windows to increase airflow.

4   Elevate the fainter's feet.
Make a pile of briefcases or file folders to a height of eight to twelve inches. Lift the fainter's feet off the floor and place them on the top of the pile.

Elevate the fainter's feet.

5 | Loosen tight clothing.
Undo the fainter's tie and/or top button
and any other restrictive clothing or
jewelry. Do not engage in excessive
clothes loosening.

6 | Attempt to awaken the fainter.
Tap him on the shoulder, saying, "Can
you hear me?" Do not slap or pour water
on the fainter.

7 | Check for vital signs.
Hold a finger two inches from the fainter's
face and feel for air entering the nose.
Lightly grasp his palm and feel for a pulse.
If the fainter has both a breath and a
pulse, skip to step 10.

8 | Deliver "rescue breaths" to the
fainting victim.
Pinch the fainter's nose closed, elevate
the chin, and open the mouth. Place your
mouth over the fainter's mouth, making a

seal. Deliver a long "rescue breath" into his mouth. If his chest begins to rise as your breath enters, skip to step 10.

9 | Perform chest compressions on the fainter.
Place your hands on top of one another at the center of the fainter's chest. Push down firmly, about two inches. Repeat this compression action 30 times in 30 seconds. Repeat steps 8 and 9 until the fainter revives, or help arrives.

10 | Let the fainter revive slowly.
Cover his forehead and neck with wet paper towels. The fainter should sit quietly as long as necessary to regain strength. Offer him water, a sports drink, or juice.

Be Aware
Signs that someone is about to faint include paleness, sweating, and frequent yawning.

INSTANT SOLUTION

DISLODGE AN AIRWAY OBSTRUCTION

Stand behind the choking coworker. Make a fist and bring it up in a swift motion into the area just above the bellybutton and below the ribs. Repeat until the victim coughs out the cookie, or other airway obstruction.

HOW TO FLATTER AN INSECURE BOSS

⭐ Sit next to your boss.

⭐ Loudly agree with your boss's statements.
Enthusiastically say "yes" to each of her suggestions and ideas. Vary your expressions of agreement to include: "I agree," "I totally agree," "I completely agree," and "I couldn't agree more." After your boss completes a declarative statement, add the word "obviously."

⭐ Silently affirm your boss's statements.
Constantly nod as your boss speaks. Smile and chuckle quietly to yourself to express how much you completely agree with what is being said.

★ | Write down everything your boss says.

★ | Duplicate your boss's food order.
When someone is taking sandwich orders, wait until after your boss has made her order, and then say "ditto," "the same," or "sounds good."

★ | Laugh at your boss's jokes.
Watch your boss's body language for signs that what she is saying is meant to be humorous, such as raised eyebrows and teeth showing. Only laugh if you are sure what your boss is saying is meant to be a joke.

★ | Take your boss's side in arguments.
When other people continue to disagree with her, roll your eyes and shush them.

★ | Ask your boss for advice.
During breaks in the meeting, ask her for counsel on work issues. Write down each

Laugh at your boss's jokes.

piece of advice and thank her profusely. During subsequent conversations, ask for advice on nonwork issues, such as romance, fashion, and family relationships.

⭐ Offhandedly compliment your boss as you exit the meeting.
As the meeting breaks up, position yourself near the doorway as your boss passes by. Remark to a coworker how enlightening/exciting you found the meeting to be. Place your compliments within a larger pattern. Make such statements such as: "Wow! Another great meeting from [boss's name]."

CHARACTERS TO WATCH OUT FOR

Character	Typical Behavior
The Naysayer	Heavy sighing; rolling eyes
The Narcissist	Leaning back in chair, hands laced behind head; smoothing down tie
The Jokester	Waggling eyebrows, smirk; tie features dogs playing poker
The Idiot	One finger twirling hair, chewing gum; late to meeting—missed the e-mail
The Stress Case	Hands running through hair; biting lower lip

Typical Comments

"We'll see, won't we. We'll just see."

"Let me offer a more eloquent solution."

"NOT"

"Wait—what?"

"OK. OK. [deep breath]. OK."

HOW TO DISCREETLY PASS GAS MID-MEETING

⭐ Cough loudly.
Cough again and get a drink of water.

⭐ Yawn and stretch vigorously.

⭐ Crinkle or tear up a piece of paper.
Show a sign of disgust as you reject the proposal written on the paper.

⭐ Applaud vigorously.
Time it correctly so that the moment is appropriate.

Applaud vigorously.

33. *Interpersonal Skills*

★ Laugh loudly.
Pound the table. Snort with laughter.

★ Move your chair to produce loud squeaking noise.

★ Drop a thick report or file on the floor.

★ Call the conference room.
Holding your cell phone under the table, dial the conference room number and the extension. Wait for the phone to ring.

★ Deflect the blame.
Glance at a colleague to your right and wrinkle your nose with distaste. Make eye contact with a colleague across the table; slightly incline your head to the right and mouth the word "whoa."

Be Aware

The techniques outlined can also be used to mask the sounds of burping, stomach growling, or coughing up phlegm.

How to Stifle Uncontrollable Laughter

⭐ Cough as you are laughing.

⭐ Stab yourself in the thigh with a pen or pencil.

⭐ Snap a binder clip closed on your finger.

⭐ Pull on your necktie.

⭐ Exit the room.
Excuse yourself and rapidly walk to the bathroom.

Multitasking Range

Acceptable	Questionable
Checking e-mail	Checking stocks
Using hand sanitizer	Using face moisturizer
Drinking water	Making iced tea
Adjusting tie	Using lint-roller
Checking makeup	Applying makeup
Eating a sandwich	Making a sandwich

Unacceptable

Playing video games

Using a loofah

Making a cocktail

Getting a haircut

Getting a manicure/pedicure

Eating lobster

Chapter 2
In the Spotlight

SHOWING UP IS HALF THE BATTLE

HOW TO FAKE YOUR WAY THROUGH A PRESENTATION

1 Speak clearly.
Do not mumble or raise your voice. Speak slowly and evenly. Act as if you are over-explaining very difficult material that the audience might not understand.

2 Stand up straight.
Project confidence with your body language. Smile and make frequent eye contact with your listeners.

3 Make up statistics.
Pepper your presentation with facts and figures. Bombard the listeners with numbers. Glance down at notes in your hand

Make up statistics. Use entertaining props.

so it appears that you are being careful to get the statistics right.

4 Scrawl.

Use a messy scrawl when writing statistics or other imaginary information on an easel or dry-erase board. Erase each number or flip the page immediately to make room for new fictional information.

5 Ask the audience questions.

Broad questions such as, "What are the results we're looking for here?" or "Who are our competitors?" or "What are the greatest risks?" will provoke numerous and varied responses. Use your presentation time to write them on the board or flip chart.

6 Use entertaining props.

Make a puppet out of a coworker's tie. Pour water from a pitcher into a glass to illustrate how capital flows into the market. Remove your blazer and wave it in front of you as if you are a toreador, taking on the bull-like challenges of a changing economy.

7 | **Give nonanswers to all questions.**
Praise the questioner ("That's a really good question. Thank you for asking that."), insult the questioner ("I don't think we need to waste time explaining that."), or say you'd like to answer but want to keep going ("That falls outside the scope of this presentation.").

8 | **Conclude with a personal anecdote.**
Change the subject from business to a story your father used to tell you. When finished, smile and raise your eyebrows enigmatically.

9 | **Exit the room.**
Say thank you and leave immediately.

THINGS NEVER TO SAY
IN A MEETING

Instead of Saying	Say
"I disagree."	"It definitely has possibilities."
"No."	"That's an interesting idea."
"That's the worst idea I've ever heard."	"Let me get back to you on that."
"Let's solve this problem right now."	"Let's schedule a follow-up meeting to discuss potential solutions."
"I will handle it."	"Let's schedule a follow-up meeting to figure out who is going to handle it."
"I'm really attracted to you."	"Let's schedule a follow-up meeting to discuss strategies for implementation."
"I am so bored right now I feel like I'm going to die."	"I have another meeting to get to."
"I am really drunk right now."	Say nothing.

INSTANT SOLUTION

TAKE THE LAST DOUGHNUT

Hold the doughnut aloft and announce "This is the last one. Does anyone want to split this with me?" Touch as much of the doughnut's surface area as possible.

HOW TO LIVEN UP A MEETING

⭐ **Schedule a dance break.**
Midway through the presentation, switch applications on your laptop to media software. Play fast, rhythmic music such as techno or disco. Have all meeting attendants dance or spin around in their rolling chairs for 30 seconds. Resume the meeting.

⭐ **Invite guest stars.**
Hire a celebrity, musician, or actor and have him wait in the hall until midway through the meeting. Throw open the door and introduce the celebrity in a booming voice. Connect the guest star's appearance to a particular agenda item. For example, "to discuss our decline in B2B marketing in the third quarter, please welcome Mr. Hulk Hogan!"

✪ Play "telephone."

Instead of making an important announcement, whisper it into the ear of the colleague to your right; that person then whispers it in the ear of the person to her right, and so on, until it makes it back around the room to you. Say both the original announcement and the "telephone" version. Vote on which version the group prefers, and act on it.

✪ Designate a fake accent day.

Assign every participant in the meeting to a different English language accent they must use throughout the meeting. Examples include Australian, Scottish, Irish, and American Deep South.

✪ Organize a murder mystery.

Arrange for the lights to suddenly go out and for a theatrical scream to be heard from the hall. When the lights go back on, have an actor dressed as a policeman enter

*Have the attendees dance or spin around in their
rolling chairs for 30 seconds.*

and announce that someone has been murdered. Declare everyone at the meeting a suspect, and say that you all must try to solve the crime, but first you must proceed through the agenda items.

★ Do "the Wave."
Starting from the person to the right of the door, each meeting participant rises one at a time and waves both hands in the air. Once the Wave has made it all the way around the conference table three times, everyone yells "whoo!" Resume meeting.

★ Announce layoffs.

★ Announce your resignation.

INSTANT SOLUTION

CREATE ATMOSPHERE

Use your laptop's media application to play smooth jazz, and set the screensaver on "Tiki Lamp." Serve coffee in wine flutes, or wine-flute shaped plastic cups.

HOW TO SHOW UP LATE TO A MEETING

⭐ **Enter quietly.**
Remove your shoes outside the door to the conference room. Crack the door and scan the room for an open seat closest to the door. When someone dims the lights to make a multimedia presentation, walk on your toes into the room and hurriedly take your seat. Put your shoes back on before the meeting is over.

⭐ **Enter tapping your watch.**
Hold your watch to your ear to hear if it's still ticking. Shrug ruefully as you sit down.

⭐ **Bring snacks.**
Enter the meeting with doughnuts and coffee, chips and dips, or bagels.

★ Hover outside the meeting room talking on your cell phone.
Pace back and forth within sight and, if possible, hearing of people at the meeting. Loudly say, "Terrific." Then walk confidently and smiling into the meeting.

★ Lower expectations.
When running 20 minutes late, call the office and have a message relayed to the meeting that you are running 45 minutes late. When you arrive, accept thanks for rushing.

★ Enter "commando style."
Lie down on your stomach just outside the entrance to the conference room, clutching your laptop to your chest. When a colleague opens the door to go to the restroom, wriggle into the room on your stomach, remaining below eye level with those inside. Climb up on and into a chair.

Crawl into the room on your stomach,
below your coworkers' line of sight.

53. *In the Spotlight*

★ Enter wheeling a cart full of files
and materials.
Create the impression that you have been
gathering vital information and just could
not stop.

★ Attend the meeting with significant
handicaps.
Enter the meeting wearing an arm-sling
or tourniquet, in a wheelchair with a full-
leg cast, or pushing an IV tube. Do not
offer any explanation for your condition.

★ Create a diversion outside the
meeting room.
Set fire to a wastepaper basket, turn
chickens loose in the hall, or otherwise
cause people to leave the meeting room.
When they return, slip in with them.

THINGS TO LOOK FOR
WHEN RETURNING FROM
THE BATHROOM

- Unzipped fly

- Untucked shirt

- Skirt on backwards or caught in underwear

- Sweat stains in underarms

- Smeared makeup

- Toilet paper stuck to shoe or dangling from pant leg

- Water accidentally splashed onto midsection from bathroom sink

- Food in teeth, on shirt, in hair

- Newspaper folded under arm with partially solved crossword puzzle

HOW TO STEAL FOCUS

⭐ Use body language.
When someone else is speaking, point at her while nodding your head in agreement. Make gestures to accompany her words; if she says a problem is large, raise both hands and hold them far apart, to illustrate the concept of largeness for the speaker.

⭐ Jump in.
Immediately start speaking as soon as anyone else stops. Literally jump out of your seat as you start.

⭐ Interrupt.
If you disagree with what is being said, do not wait until the speaker has finished; begin your rebuttal loudly and immediately. If you agree with what's being said,

Announce your agreement immediately and loudly.

57. *In the Spotlight*

announce your agreement immediately
and loudly.

★ Take everything to heart.
Greet any information as if it is of vital
importance to you, personally. When sales
figures are down, put your head in your
hands and sigh heavily. When a colleague
announces a successful sales event, pump
your fist in the air and shout, "Yes! YES!"

★ Get up a lot.
While you are speaking, stand up and
pace back and forth, gesturing vigorously.
While someone else is speaking, stand
up and pace back and forth, gesturing
vigorously.

★ Laugh loudly.
No matter the quality of the speaker's
joke, lean back in your seat and bray
with laughter.

NONCOMMITTAL AFFIRMATIONS

"That's a really interesting idea."

"I see where you're going."

"Could work. Could definitely work."

"In a perfect world, yes."

"It bears thinking about."

"Ah."

"Let's turn that over for a bit."

"Why don't you take that idea and see where it goes."

"If it were up to me, yes."

"Let me run that up the flag pole."

HOW TO KEEP A MEETING SHORT

⭐ Schedule the meeting when limited time is available.
Book the conference room for a half-hour block, at a time when another meeting is scheduled to begin immediately thereafter.

⭐ Provide fewer chairs than there are participants.
Inform those without chairs that they must stand or sit on the floor.

⭐ Stick to the agenda.
Distribute the agenda in advance and have it available at the meeting.

⭐ Slowly turn up the heat over the course of the meeting.

★ Provide beverages.
Encourage meeting participants to drink several cups of coffee and/or bottles of water over the course of the meeting. When people rise to go to the restroom, look at your watch and say, "We're almost finished; can you wait a couple minutes?"

★ Encourage agreement.
People who raise concerns or have criticism should be silenced. Tell them they need to be positive and constructive. Disagreement and careful deliberation can take a lot of time.

★ While a long-winded person is speaking, rapidly drum your fingers on the table in front of you.
Repeat.

Provide fewer chairs than there are participants.

⭐ Raise your wrist to chest height and glance at your watch. Elevate the opposite hand and vigorously rub your eyes. Repeat.

⭐ Flatten the fingers of your right hand over your thumb to make a "mouth"; rapidly open and shut the mouth ("yap yap yap"). Repeat.

⭐ Raise your forefinger and rapidly twirl it in a circle ("wrap it up"). Repeat.

⭐ Postpone difficult decisions for a later meeting. When an agenda item looks like it will be time consuming, schedule the issue for future consideration. Appoint a committee to look into the issue.

CHAPTER 3
UNDERACHIEVEMENT

CHECKING OUT

HOW TO STAY AWAKE DURING A MEETING

⭐ Drink several ultra-caffeinated energy drinks.
Begin ninety minutes before the meeting starts.

⭐ Sit in an uncomfortable chair.
Look for a seat that is missing its cushion and has a broken leg or wheel. Place an uncomfortable object such as a binder clip underneath you before you sit down.

⭐ Poke yourself in the thigh with a pen.
Unclick the pen so the nib is not exposed. Press the tip into your leg a quarter inch, until you feel the sharp pinch but before the skin is broken.

Poke yourself in the thigh with your pen.

⭐ Drink coffee.
Alternate between cups of coffee and bottles of water throughout the meeting.

⭐ Do not go to the bathroom.
Keep your bladder full to prevent you from drifting off.

⭐ Set your cell phone on vibrate.
Leave instructions for friends and associates to call and e-mail you during the scheduled meeting time. Leave the phone in your pocket so it is in contact with your leg, where you will be irritated by the buzz of incoming calls and e-mails.

⭐ Think about upsetting things.
Ruminate on aspects of your life that are causing you anxiety, such as the failure of intimate relationships, the number of unpaid bills you have, or the possibility of natural disasters.

★ Think of opposing arguments.
For every point or suggestion, come up with a contrarian position.

★ Take notes in a foreign language.

★ Take notes with your nondominant hand.

★ Participate in the meeting.
Answer and ask questions. Volunteer to help with presentations. Contribute to group discussions.

Buzzwords to Use in a Pinch

- 2.0
- B2B, B2C, B2B v. B2C
- Bandwidth
- Bleeding edge
- Contextualize, Decontextualize, Recontextualize
- Cross-platform
- Customer-centric
- De-incent
- Enterprise
- Facilitate
- Framework
- Incent
- Offline
- Paradigm shift
- Skill set
- Synergize
- Touch base
- Value-added
- Win-Win

HOW TO SURVIVE PHOTOCOPYING MISHAPS

STAPLED FINGER

1 Remove the staple.
Use tweezers to grasp the emerging end of the staple and yank it out in one clean motion.

2 Stop the bleeding.
Stick your finger in your mouth and suck on the wound until bleeding stops.

3 Determine if you need a tetanus shot.
If you are uncertain of the age or origin of the staple, or whether you have had a tetanus shot within the last five years, leave the meeting and go to the hospital.

Underachievement

TONER STAINS ON CLOTHES

1 Splash the stain with cold water.
Use the faucet in the meeting room
sink, or a water pitcher, to douse the
affected garment.

2 Spray with hairspray.
Thoroughly spray the stained area with
aerosol hairspray. Ink stains respond well
to alcohol.

3 Blot.
Use wadded napkins or paper towels to
blot the stain. Do not rub, which will
spread the stain around. Instead, repeat-
edly press down with the napkins/towels
and release.

4 Let the stain dry.
If appropriate, remove the garment and
sling it over a chair until it dries.

Apply aerosol hairspray to the toner-stained areas.

73.   *Underachievement*

FINGER CAUGHT IN A SLAMMED COPY-MACHINE DOOR

1 Determine if the finger is broken.
Signs of a broken finger include swelling, sharp pain in the joints, bruising/bleeding, and a lumpy or misshapen appearance.

2 Improvise a splint.
Tie or tape the injured finger to a nail file or bundle of coffee stirrers to keep it immobile.

3 Ice the finger.
Avoid swelling by pressing a handful of ice wrapped in a napkin against the affected hand.

4 Use your other hand to complete the copies.

INSTANT SOLUTION

FIX A WOBBLY CONFERENCE TABLE

Crouch under the table and shake it back and forth to determine which leg is short. Place a report you have not referred to for at least six months under the short leg to wedge it level.

HOW TO ESCAPE FROM A MEETING ROOM

★ Create a distraction.
Use a handheld device with Internet access to order a large food delivery, balloon bouquet, or stripper-gram to the conference room. When the delivery or performer arrives, slip out in the confusion.

★ Go check on something at your desk.
When asked for a piece of information, explain that the answer is at your desk; get up to fetch it and never return. If asked later, say that while you were away a call came in that you had to take.

★ **Fake a telephone call.**
Use an automated application to cause
your own phone to ring midmeeting.
Look at the incoming call number with
an expression of urgent concern and stand
up. Mouth "I'm so sorry" to the other
attendees as you hurry from the room.

★ **Set off the carbon monoxide alarm.**
Nonchalantly lean way back in your seat
and press the "test" button on the carbon
monoxide alarm, causing the shrill,
piercing alarm to go off.

★ **Become too aggravated to continue.**
When someone makes a disagreeable suggestion or presents bad news, throw your
arms up, shake your head in exaggerated
frustration, and leave the room. Do not
use this technique at more than two meetings in a row.

Ride out with the leftovers.

ESCAPE ON A CATERING CART

1 Wait until the food has been brought in and unloaded.

2 Linger at the catering cart.
Sip a cup of coffee. Look casual.

3 Wait until the attendees have returned to their tables and the meeting has resumed.

4 Crouch on the ground.
Tip your plate over so your food spills onto the carpet. Bend over to pick it up and remain on the ground.

5 Climb onto the cart.
Spread aside the tablecloth covering the bottom of the cart. Climb fully inside the catering cart, and pull the tablecloth closed around you.

6 Ride out with the leftovers.

Underachievement

SEATING ARRANGEMENT CHART

Where You Are	What It Means
In front of everyone	You are the boss.
Next to the boss	You are the boss's favorite, or you are the boss's assistant.
Across from the boss/ Next to overhead projector	You are the boss's favorite, or you are considered to be good at fixing the overhead projector when it breaks.
Two seats down from the boss	The boss hasn't made up his mind about you, or is unaware of you.
Three seats down from the boss	You are considered of uncertain importance and/or you have a body odor problem.
Four seats down from the boss, by the door	You are considered of marginal importance and will be asked to go get lunch for everyone.
Standing	You are of no importance.

HOW TO MAKE AN ORIGAMI HAT

1 Take your copy of the meeting agenda and fold it in half.
Run your thumb along the midline crease until it becomes crisp.

2 Fold the top right corner of the meeting agenda towards the middle.

3 Fold the top left corner of the meeting agenda towards the middle.
Run your thumb along each of these folds, so they are crisp. Your copy of the meeting agenda should now look like an isosceles triangle above a long rectangular base.

4 Fold the facing flap at the bottom of the meeting agenda up towards the middle.

5 Flip the entire meeting agenda over.

Underachievement

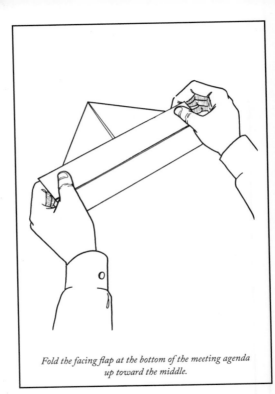

Fold the facing flap at the bottom of the meeting agenda up toward the middle.

6 | Flip the flap of the back of the meeting agenda up towards the middle.

7 | Do not put on your hat.
Wait until the meeting is over to play with your origami hat.

Be Aware

Any rectangular size of paper will work. For a hat that will fit on most adult-sized heads, use legal-size paper or larger.

INSTANT SOLUTION

ENTERTAIN YOURSELF DURING A MEETING

Open a binder in front of you on the table. Behind this barricade, do puzzles, or draw pictures of your officemates as though wearing clown makeup.

HOW TO VIDEO-CONFERENCE FROM THE BEACH

1. **Dress your upper body appropriately.**
Wear a shirt, buttoned all the way up. Add a necktie, sweater, or blazer over the shirt. Shave and/or put on makeup. Brush and comb your hair. Remove sunglasses or goggles. Remove zinc oxide and suntan lotion from the bridge of your nose.

2. **Keep your lower body out of the frame.**
Before linking to the meeting, zoom the digital video camera in tightly, so that you can only be seen from your ribcage up.

3. **Employ props.**
Hold a pen. Once every five or ten minutes, tap it thoughtfully against your chin. Clutch papers in your hand and occasionally bring

Underachievement

Keep your lower body out of the frame. Employ props.

them up into the frame; when they are
not in the frame, occasionally rustle them.
Pour your pina colada into a coffee cup
and periodically sip it (remove the straw).

4 | Create a background.
Take cushions from lounge chairs and prop
them up behind you, creating the impression that you are sitting on a sofa. If you
have called in sick, scatter a thermometer,
hot water bottle, a tissue box, and aspirin
containers around the cushions.

5 | Wear a microphone.
Clip a cheap microphone to your collar,
as close as possible to your mouth to
drown out any stray background noise,
such as waves crashing on the beach, or
children laughing.

6 | Participate in the meeting.

7 Sit up straight.
Leaning to one side will reveal the panoramic ocean vista.

8 Do not fall asleep.
If you drift off, you may slump out of frame and reveal your tropical surroundings.

9 Experience technical problems.
With your big toe, reach forward and shut off your laptop.

10 Go for a swim.

11 Send an e-mail to your boss.
Explain that your connection must have been lost. Apologize. Ask that someone send you information on what you missed from the rest of the meeting.

12 Go for another swim.

INDEX

ACKNOWLEDGMENTS

David Borgenicht would like to thank Sarah O'Brien, Steve Mockus, Jenny Kraemer, Brenda Brown, and Ben Winters for making this book happen. In gratitude, he proclaims the next book "meeting free."

Ben H. Winters would like to thank his new friends at the U.S. Department of Labor, whose raised eyebrows he could see over the phone; and especially all his friends and colleagues with "real" jobs, the kind that involve putting on pants, going to places, and talking to people.

ABOUT THE AUTHORS

David Borgenicht is the creator and coauthor of all the books in the *Worst-Case Scenario* series, and is president and publisher of Quirk Books (www.irreference.com). He has never passed gas midmeeting, but he's pretty sure the guy next to him did. He lives in Philadelphia.

Ben H. Winters lives in Brooklyn, New York, where he writes plays, books, and articles. He holds a black belt in taking the last doughnut. You can have a meeting with Ben by visiting www.BenHWinters.com.

Brenda Brown is an illustrator and cartoonist whose work has been published in many books and publications, including the *Worst-Case Scenario* series, *Esquire*, *Reader's Digest*, *USA Weekend*, *21st Century Science & Technology*, the *Saturday Evening Post*, and the *National Enquirer*. Her Web site is www.webtoon.com.

MORE WORST-CASE SCENARIO PRODUCTS

VISIT THESE WEBSITES FOR MORE WORST-CASE SCENARIO PRODUCTS:

- ✪ Board games
  www.universitygames.com
- ✪ Gadgets
  www.protocoldesign.com
- ✪ Mobile
  www.namcogames.com
- ✪ Posters and puzzles
  www.aquariusimages.com/wcs.html

For updates, new scenarios, and more, visit:
www.worstcasescenarios.com

To order books visit:
www.chroniclebooks.com/worstcase

MORE WORST-CASE SCENARIOS

HANDBOOKS

- ✪ The Worst-Case Scenario Survival Handbook
- ✪ Travel
- ✪ Dating & Sex
- ✪ Golf
- ✪ Holidays
- ✪ Work
- ✪ College
- ✪ Weddings
- ✪ Parenting
- ✪ Extreme Edition
- ✪ Life

ALMANACS

- ✪ History
- ✪ Great Outdoors
- ✪ Politics

CALENDARS

- ✪ Daily Survival Calendar
- ✪ Daily Survival Calendar: Golf

POCKET GUIDES

- ✪ Dogs
- ✪ Breakups
- ✪ Retirement
- ✪ New York City
- ✪ Cats
- ✪ Meetings
- ✪ San Francisco
- ✪ Cars